COBRA AND SHELBY MUSTANG

1962-2007 PHOTO ARCHIVE

Including Prototypes and Clones

Wallace A. Wyss

Iconografix

Iconografix
PO Box 446
Hudson, Wisconsin 54016 USA

The information in this book is true and complete to the best of our knowledge. All recommendations are made without any guarantee on the part of the author or Publisher, who also disclaim any liability incurred in connection with the use of this data or specific details.

We acknowledge that certain words, such as model names and designations, mentioned herein are the property of the trademark holder. We use them for purposes of identification only. This is not an official publication.

Iconografix books are offered at a discount when sold in quantity for promotional use. Businesses or organizations seeking details should write to the Marketing Department, Iconografix, at the above address.

Library of Congress Control Number: 2007927571

ISBN-10: 1-58388-198-0
ISBN-13: 978-1-58388-198-9

07 08 09 10 11 12 6 5 4 3 2 1

Printed in China

Cover and book design by Dan Perry

Copyediting by Suzie Helberg

Cover photo-Early Cobra updated. When Lynn Park, Cobra maven extraordinaire, bought this Cobra he found that it had been a 260 up-dated to a 289 under the hood and side vents added. Color is close to the color of CSX2000, the very first Cobra that Shelby had painted Candy Pearl Yellow by customizer Dean Jeffries.

BOOK PROPOSALS

Iconografix is a publishing company specializing in books for transportation enthusiasts. We publish in a number of different areas, including Automobiles, Auto Racing, Buses, Construction Equipment, Emergency Equipment, Farming Equipment, Railroads & Trucks. The Iconografix imprint is constantly growing and expanding into new subject areas.

Authors, editors, and knowledgeable enthusiasts in the field of transportation history are invited to contact the Editorial Department at Iconografix, Inc., PO Box 446, Hudson, WI 54016.

www.iconografixinc.com

Acknowledgments

Special thanks to John Clinard of Ford Motor Co., SAAC stalwarts and fact checkers Ned Scudder and Jeff Burgy and Cobra restorer Mike McCluskey. Thanks also to the photographers who generously donated from their archives.

Preface

As a teenager, I always lusted after Shelby Cobras and GT40s. During the summers of my high school years, I repaired sprinkler control timers in Kansas City and as part of my job, got into some of the most exclusive garages in the city. It was during this period that I saw my first Cobra and GT40, the very cars that I read about in the various car magazines of that era.

Fast forward to the mid 1980s after I started my first data storage company, I finally had the means to purchase a few vintage cars and go racing. But I chose poorly and purchased a vintage Ferrari, went to Bondurant's racing school, and subsequently got blown away on the track by Cobras. History does repeat itself. It was during this period that I met Bill Murray of Murray Racing in Longmont, Colorado. Bill successfully raced Cobras in SCCA and had a premier race prep and restoration shop. Bill helped me acquire my first factory team Cobra and we went vintage racing together. We also became close friends. I subsequently moved to Boulder, Colorado, with my family and started a series of high tech companies. As my collection of Shelby Cobras, GT40s, and Shelby Mustangs grew, space became a concern. I had also acquired a large amount of Shelby memorabilia from a collector that had planned to create a museum in Texas.

In 1996, Bill Murray, his brother Dave, and I decided we had enough critical mass with the other Shelby automobile collectors we raced with to start a museum. So I purchased a building, set up a non-profit operating foundation, and the Shelby-American Collection opened its doors in December of 1996. It is the finest collection of Shelby racecars and memorabilia in the world and it is the only collection of its type that is dedicated to the accomplishments of Carroll Shelby and the Shelby-American Team in the 1960s. It has also been very fulfilling to work with Carroll Shelby and the drivers, mechanics, photographers, etc. that worked for Shelby in the 1960s who have become involved in our museum effort.

In opening the collection for public viewing, we have hosted a number of significant events such as book signings and charity functions—inviting as guests of honor many of the famous personalities of the Shelby-American era from Dan Gurney, Phil Hill, Jack Sears and Bob Bondurant and many others to Shelby himself who is a regular attendee. Much was learned about the life and times of these gentlemen during what is called "The Glory Days of the Sixties." When Wallace Wyss told me he was doing a picture book about Cobras and Shelby Mustangs, I told me we would like to share some of the facts about our cars. For those who haven't yet had an opportunity to visit the collection, this is a chance to see what the cars were like then, and how some Cobras look now, with 40 years or more on the clock. We also actively race many of the cars in the collection at various tracks in the U.S. and Europe. I hope you will stop by and see us if you are ever in Boulder. You can visit our website at www.shelbyamericancollection.org.

While I realize that this is a picture book, I hope some of my enthusiasm shows through. I feel that you can't help but be enthusiastic when you hear the story of Shelby, a former chicken farmer from East Texas, and how he took on the sports car world and won its premier race, the 24 Hours of Le Mans, in addition to the World Manufacturers' Championship. These pictures show some of his creations and I hope, like me, you'll become a fan….

Steve Volk
Shelby-American Collection
Boulder, Colorado

Foreword

My first association with Cobras came back in 1962, when I read about Shelby and his new car in the car magazines and hot-footed it down to Princeton Ave. in Venice to see what the fuss was all about.

I wanted to buy one but they were a little steep for me at the time so I bought an A.C. Aceca instead and did my own backyard Cobra, dropping in a 289. I received advice from Shelby employees.

Later, after I came back from the Army in 1969, I was able to buy my first Cobra.

Thus began one of life's great adventures. I bought more Cobras as my career proceeded and my family would allow it (thanks, dear wife and kids for indulging me). I joined the Cobra Owner's Club and have attended meetings for over 35 years. I eventually got into big blocks but never sold my small blocks so now I have some of the most interesting examples of each and can convince you on the virtues of either.

Which one's better? I will say that a small block set up right can give a big block a hard time.

Throughout the years I collected magazine articles and took many pictures, a couple of which you see here.

I was a bit shocked when Steve Arntz cloned a Cobra and, like Shelby, was righteously indignant at the sacrilege. However, time passed and the original Cobras soared in price (now selling your average 427 Cobra would buy you a five-bedroom home in Memphis, maybe even with a view of the river).

They became unaffordable to young enthusiasts. A whole generation was going to miss the fun of discovering the Cobra because of the prices of the originals. So I came to accept the clones and even became a supplier for them. By the way, Shelby eventually came around to welcoming the new younger generation and now sells a wide variety of clones.

Now as far as Ford Motor Company, I was as pleased as punch that Ford and Shelby buried the hatchet and are working together again. I am happy with the new Ford GT and it looks like the '07 Shelby GT500 will be a real barnstormer.

I am hoping either, or both, of the Ford Concept Cobras makes it to production. There's a willing group of buyers out there. I am torn between the old and the new, though maybe, at my age, I have decided to stick with the old.

I hope you find this book interesting. I know at my wheel company I'd get a dozen calls a day from guys asking about little details like, "Did the 427 road cars have a hood scoop?" I hope some of these pictures answer your questions.

On the other hand, Shelby being Shelby (and I have to admit that is part of the fun of reading Shelby history), he made little variations in the cars he built, some to slip by the racing regs and some just because maybe he got bored. His own 427 Cobra, for instance, had twin superchargers and produced something like 600 horsepower. And get this—it was an automatic!

I wish there could have been more in this book on the team members and factory employees but this is a book just about the cars. I must say that part of enjoying the Shelby-American legend is all the great people I have met who were with the original company way back when.

Every time I drive my Cobras, I remember them and hope we are building the legend.

Lynn Park
La Crecenta, California

Introduction

I confess that as an idle youth I, like many Detroiters, cruised Woodward Avenue night after night, usually riding shotgun in Bob Blossom's Triumph TR-3. Era? We're talkin' 'round 1960-65.

From the Big Boy down by Nine Mile we headed North to the Totem Pole, then to Ted's. It was 'round and 'round we went. A million times. A thousand nights.

We saw a lot of interesting cars, even acid-dipped Mopars running 426 Hemis, Ford Thunderbolts, modified Pontiacs from Ace Wilson's Royal Pontiac, even a customized prewar Mercedes being driven by GM VP William L. Mitchell, a genuine certified boy racer.

But the car we loved to see most was a dead stock white 289 Cobra driven by a local Royal Oak car dealer. He would get out there and run against anything that pulled up at the light.

We were there, in Detroit, when the whole Cobra thing was happening. But, busy at the time with college, I caught only glimpses, like the time I saw the Cobra Caravan come through Detroit or the time I saw "Gentleman" Tom Payne in a Cobra thrash an E-type Jaguar at Waterford Hills Road Racing course (I think Stirling Moss was at the wheel of the E-type; its freeze plug blew).

I wasn't to learn more about Cobras until 1965 when I worked for *Motor Trend* and went out to the Shelby-American factory to do a story on the new 427 Cobra. The public relations man offered me a test car but my superior turned it down (Mike Lamm, how could you?).

Now, 40-plus years later, I still find myself catching up on the cars made during the original Shelby years. I think this book covers most of them, though there are the one-offs made for various and sundry personages, or the prototypes (like the Green Hornet notchback) that were supposed to be destroyed but somehow survived.

Since the '70s, there's this whole industry that has sprung up to try to recapture the magic of those golden years—replica Cobras and now, lately, replica Shelby Mustangs, some of each made by the ol' Snakemeister himself.

When I went through my archives, I tried to select as many pictures as I could of the original cars, so the guys with the replicas can see what the originals looked like way back when and maybe bring their cars a little closer to what I saw in the 1960s. And I offer a glimpse too of the new cars that Ford keeps tantalizing us with—like the Cobra Concept roadster and Cobra Concept GR-1 coupe.

Ford delivered of course on the 2007 Shelby GT500 (plus surprised us with the GT-H model and Shelby GT model) but hasn't yet green-lighted a modern two seater Cobra. Still, hope springs eternal. Ford's going through some big changes now and, as much as we would like it, they can't rely just on performance cars (though we thank them eternally for the new Ford GT). Shelby's involved, as much as you can be at 84 years old. Remarkably, he's still at it, foot to the floor.

Wallace Wyss
Cobra Ranch
Mendocino, California
January 2007

Around 1954, Carroll Hall Shelby, a failed East Texas chicken farmer, came out of nowhere (actually Leesburg, Texas) and in short order took the sports car world by storm as a hot driver (his nickname was "the Texas tornado"). Early in the 1950s, U.S. racing organizations still didn't allow sports car drivers to be awarded cash prizes. Over in Europe drivers got paid. Shelby went to Europe as early as 1954 in search of a "factory ride," which he got from Aston Martin. He raced nearly 50 different marques before he hung up his driving gloves and helmet at the end of the 1960 season, sidelined by a heart ailment that went back to a childhood bout with rheumatic fever. Here he's shown around 1956 at Pomona, California, in a Maserati and a Ferrari, state-of-the-art Italian cars supplied by wealthy California-based sponsors. *Author's collection, D. Brandel photos*

Shelby at first had to go to Europe to find "factory rides" from companies like Aston Martin because in the U.S. amateur racing was amateur, i.e. no prize money. But by the mid-'50s, he was able to land wealthy sponsors in the U.S. who would pay him to drive the finest Ferraris and Maseratis they could get from Italy. Here, in a Ferrari numbered 141, he lines up on the grid at Montgomery, New York, in '56. Also on the grid we see two gullwing Mercedes, a Porsche 550 and a Maserati. *Ozzie Lyons*

Yes, indeed, Shelby was a racer before he was a car builder. And before that he was a chicken farmer, cement contractor, test pilot (during WWII), flight instructor, oil field roughneck, and on and on. In the mid-'50s he met two high roller sponsors, first Tony Parravano, then John Edgar. Both bought the finest Ferraris and Maseratis money could buy and Shelby piloted them to dozens of victories in 1956 and 1957, though his high point as a driver was winning the 24 Hours of Le Mans for Aston Martin in 1959, partnered with British co-driver Roy Salvadori. Shelby is shown here in car number 5 just pulling out onto the track in an Aston Martin DBR1. It didn't matter that he didn't jump into the lead right off because, 24 hours later, he was first across the finish line.

Here's a little capsule history on how the A.C. Cobra body style evolved. In the beginning, and we're talking 1949 here, there was the Ferrari 166 "Barchetta" (meaning "little boat") designed by Carlo Felice Bianchi Anderloni for Carrozzeria Touring. It was a body style copied by British specials makers creating a sort of "poor man's Ferrari."

A.C. Cars Ltd. suddenly realized in the early 1950s that their entire car line was what the Brits called "redundant," i.e., totally obsolete. So once they saw a Tojiero special, built by freelance engineer John Tojiero, one of several that copied the Ferrari Barchetta styling, they talked one owner into selling them his Tojiero to use as a prototype and restyled it, introducing it in 1953 as the A.C. Ace. Shown here is one of the Tojieros that inspired the Ace. At first their production A.C. Ace had an A.C.-built engine that was already ancient so the Ace didn't get a reputation as a zingy sports car until they installed the Bristol six to create the A.C. Bristol. Just before Shelby came along, A.C. had found a stopgap solution to the Bristol engine cut-off by slipping in the Ford Zephyr inline-six, displacing 2.6 liters. Because the replacement engine was lower profile than the Bristol six, they could lower the hoodline and extend the nose, and created a little known model in the A.C. 2.6 that looked remarkably like the car that became the first Cobra. Less than 40 of the A.C. 2.6 Zephyr-powered cars were sold, with dealer/racer Ken Rudd offering various hop-up versions marketed as Ruddspeed packages.

Here are two A.C-Bristols. Like the first A.C. Ace, it was a very loose interpretation of the Ferrari Barchetta body styling set atop a twin tube frame designed by John Tojiero, a Brit of Portuguese extraction. Tojiero got the idea of using transverse leaf springs from some prewar Fiat Topolinos. A.C. powerplants varied but one of the more successful used a Bristol six, a prewar design licensed by Bristol from BMW.

Top right: Shelby in 1962 in SCS2000. Ford always wanted him pictured in suit, though Pete Brock, his first ad writer, would write ads reminding people of Shel's early days as a driver, when he wore bib overalls

An early 260 Cobra, recognized by the fact that it has no side air vents. The early ones had worm and sector steering which Shelby gave up on after the first 75 cars, eventually switching to rack and pinion. *Pete Brock photo*

Lean-as-a-rail Carroll Shelby and a mechanic examine the engine installation in the first Cobra ever built. Shelby had tested the prototype in England with a 221-ci V-8 but by the time the car was shipped to Shelby at his rented digs at Dean Moon's shop in Santa Fe Springs, California, Ford had already decided the 221-ci V-8 wasn't big enough and shipped him two 260-ci versions. It was one of those that went into CSX2000. Shelby immediately began massaging it to get more power. Soon after this picture was taken, he took the car to Dearborn at the invitation of Lee Iacocca to put on a dog-and-pony show for Ford dealers. Orders poured in and he was off to the races. *Petersen Publishing photo*

Thames-Ditton England, early '60s. The A.C. factory at Thames-Ditton, was, shall we say, antiquated. Cars didn't move down the line automatically, you pushed them further on down when your bit was done. The car in the lead still has its Serial Number visible so somewhere there's an AC Cobra small block owner who can point to this picture and say "Hey, there's my car being born."

The most famous Le Mans racing Cobra, street licensed in the UK as 39PH, continued its racing career long after Le Mans, always in England. Evan Gamblin shot this photograph. Note how the car later had a spoiler affixed.

Le Mans 1963. The other Shelby-American team car. The dynamic duo had aluminum hardtops bolted on to give them better aerodynamics than the open car, which, aerodynamically, had a drag co-efficient little better than your basic brick. There was a secret to the use of the hardtop. Note the official touching the gas cap. Underneath that was a filler tube going down to the tank. Shelby made sure the filler tube was at least four inches wide so it'd hold a couple of gallons not counted in the gas tank total. Can you spot Shelby in the picture? He's wearing the baseball hat and light jacket, trying to go incognito, not so easy when he won the same race four years before.

Another early car at Riverside, California. The very early cars did not have side vents. The first side vents were tried on the 1963 Le Mans cars though the ones adopted for production were a bit smaller than those on the Le Mans cars.

Carroll Shelby with his first three FIA racecars in Venice, California. Actually Shelby was far short of having enough to homologate the car (100 had to be built for the FIA to rule it a production car), but the FIA granted him homologation figuring that, with a money power like Ford behind him, all it would take is Ford pressing "button A" and the Cobras would be cranked out. *Pete Brock photo*

Two views of an almost dead stock 289 Cobra. Note the non-stock "trick" headlamps and the stock full bumper guarding the tender grille cavity. This one has the optional chrome plated wire wheels.

Los Angeles Shelby plant, 1965—two Faces of the Cobra 289. In the foreground is the competition version of the Cobra 289. Alongside it is the popular street model, produced with an automatic transmission option as well as the standard 4-speed gearbox. Note how doors on competition model are cut back further, leading to the appellation "cut-back door" model. You can tell this race car is Mile's personal racing Cobra by the British Racing Drivers' Club sticker on the door. He was very proud of being a British expatriate. *Shelby-American, Inc.*

Le Mans 1963. Ed Hugus, a veteran racer (and a WWII veteran paratrooper whose first arrival in France was by jumping out of an airplane during the invasion of Normandy) runs around the car for a driver change. Two A.C. Cobras were run that year but not as Shelby-American entries. One finished 7th overall, not bad for a brand new marque. *Ford Motor Co. photograph*

Question: Why are there so many white and blue color schemes on Cobras? Answer: Because back when Shelby was first racing in the 1950s each country was "assigned" a color for their racecars according to country. The Brits were assigned British Racing Green, the Germans silver, the Italians red, etc. By the 1960s this rule had lapsed but Pete Brock had the idea of honoring the old rule; specifically the Cunningham entries at Le Mans from the 1950s, but reversing it, making it white stripes on blue for the Shelby factory race Cobras. Some private Cobra racers still went for the Cunningham team's blue stripes on white, though that was also the theme adopted for the Shelby GT350 Mustang.

Monterey Historic. Again the classic configuration—Guardsman Blue paint, white side exhausts, chrome roll bar. This owner prefers to have a nose-down attitude, as Cobras do tend to lift their noses at speed. Few owners, though, would despoil the sacred original lines with a front spoiler.

For some Cobra owners, it's where you go that's important and this owner has followed rallying practice of the 1950s by attaching a dash plaque of each meet he attended. That can make the dash pretty crowded if you go to a lot of events.

If you liked sports car racing in the late 1950s and early 1960s, your hero was undoubtedly the tall, blonde, and handsome Daniel Sexton Gurney. Gurney was adept at racing anything—including the Cobra-powered Lotus he's standing next to—one he ordered special from Lotus—or, equally well, the hulking Galaxie behind him. Some theorize it was Shelby who retained Gurney specifically to play the role of "jackrabbit" at big events, running his Lotus out ahead of Ferraris in order to tempt them into breaking so as to pave the way for his Cobras. But his longtime mechanic, Phil Remington (who joined Gurney's company after Shelby-American dropped out of racing) says, "No, it wasn't Shelby who was telling him to do that. Dan always thought he could win." We also show the car as it runs in vintage racing today. *Ford Motor Co. photograph*

Ed Leslie was a Cobra team driver early on. A WWII veteran like Shelby (flying bombers), he was also a car dealer. Leslie and a couple of other older drivers kidded Shelby by having jackets made for the older guys like he and Miles, the jackets saying, "Old Man's Club" because the wearers of were a decade older than most of Shelby's other drivers. Note flaring on the wheelwells to meet the rules about body extending out to cover width of tires. Leslie was faster in a King Cobra. *Photo courtesy Riverside Raceway*

A very early Cobra, possibly one of the six "Le Mans replicas" Shelby made after the first two ran at Le Mans in 1963. They were notable for having wheel well flares added to the front and for having bottom-hinged, shorter trunk lids so you could open them even with the hardtop added. Wheels were pin-drive Halibrands, stronger than the wire wheels. Note no side vents.

Many musicians came dancing to the tune of the Cobra's staccato exhaust, among them, pictured here, Bob Shane of the Kingston Trio, an American folk song group. Also owning Cobras were Jimmy Webb, composer, and Herbie Hancock, jazz musician. *Pete Brock photo*

Meadowdale International Raceway June 1964. Sometimes the small block Cobras had to have a little emergency bodywork in order to meet the rules about the body covering the tires, which explains the odd bodywork behind the front wheels. This was a car run by by Dan Gerber, an independent entry. It was called the "Prune Mush Special" because Dan's family was famous for marketing baby food. Mike Odell shot this in June, 1964 at the Road America June Sprints on his trusty Canon using Kodachrome film. *Mike Odell, SportsRacingLtd.com*

427 Cobra? No, 289 FIA car. License plate reveals it is a 289 though sometimes it's hard to tell when the competition 289s had fenders almost as wide as 427 big-block Cobras. In fact the big-block body was just adapted from the 289 FIA comp car with a little width added to the fenders. One clue this is a small block is that the pipes come out from under the body instead of through the side as on a competition 427 or S/C. "Dimples" in the trunk lid were added by Shelby to accommodate the FIA suitcase since Grand Touring cars all had to be able to hold the sample suitcase provided by the FIA in order to meet the rules for GT cars.

A dead stock 289 Cobra. Ned Scudder, La Jolla-based register of Cobras for the Shelby-American Automobile Club, feels that more and more owners of real A.C. Cobras will be taking off the race equipment added by later owners and returning to the way their cars were sold new.

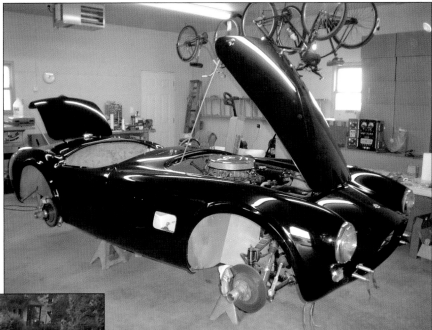

Get a good look because it's one of the last original 289 A.C. Cobras still being driven on the road. CSX 2393 belongs to expatriate Brit T.E.Warth Esq., rare car book dealer from Minnesota, who has driven almost coast to coast from his home to Shelby conventions in Philadelphia and Portland. He has owned the car since 1974 and the odometer shows over 100,000 miles which to his mind is "just broken in." Future plans include a drive to Texas in November 2007 to drive in one of the rallies that have sprung up around the country for those with genuine vintage sports cars. These rallies, such as the Colorado Grand, are fitting in that they allow the cars' owners to use the cars in the way their builders originally intended, plus see some fine sights in the meantime. Original invoice dated August 1964 to Burton Motors of Sacramento from Shelby-American Inc shows a dealer price of $5,474.05, car in silver and red (now black and red) and Group "A" Accessories. Car has 3.77 rear end.

Palm Springs, California, during the late 1980s. Shelby was at this event and must have been pleased to see one of the earliest Cobras still racing. Among the novel features is the chrome hood and tail badge that Shelby devised to cover up the holes once he'd pried off the stylized A.C. badge. It grinded Shelby that A.C. put its name everywhere, even on the pedals, which he never bothered to change.

Nurburgring 1964. A 1964 289 team car at speed. This is a revealing picture because it shows how slanted the windscreen was. That was a favorite trick of the Cobra team—they would have the car scrutinized by officials, with the windshield closer to vertical, and then pull it down once they got out on the track. But the car still had the aerodynamics of a brick! The Ring was too hard on the Cobras. It wasn't the 18-mile-long length and over 170 turns that was daunting; it was the fact that in at least four places you got airborne and Cobras did not take well to landings.

The Monterey Historic Automobile Races in 2005. This is an FIA road-racing 289 Cobra, prepared to meet FIA regulations. The driver has all the original decals except he added one for Wild West racers, a team of California-based vintage racers who would regularly bring their cars to the East Coast to teach the Easterners what hard driving was all about.

The 2005 Fontana, California, Shelby-American Automobile Club (SAAC) Meet. Yes, that's a right drive Cobra and, yes, that is a fastback hardtop like the factory team cars had but this one eschews the gas cap because modern drivers don't much care for having a plastic tube full of gasoline right behind them in case of an accident.

A USRRC racer. Though it looks at first glance like a 427 Cobra it is in fact a small block but you can see how, after they widened the rear fenders for bigger wheels and tires, it gave them the model for the later big block body style. Note coil spring retainers holding rear decklid shut. USRRC stood for "United States Road Racing Championship."

The dashboard of two Cobra roadsters, basically the same layout with two large gauges—a speedo and tach—and several smaller ones. Originally the supplier was Smiths, in England, but at some point Shelby either got a better deal from American instrument maker Stewart-Warner or figured he'd play one firm against the other in order to get their prices down, just as he did with other suppliers like steering wheel manufacturers. Early Cobras had Ford Rotunda tachs, manufactured by Faria. Later they had a Smiths reading to a heady 10,000 rpm, an unreachable peak for a Cobra engine.

Sicily 1964, the Targa Florio. Daniel Sexton Gurney, America's barefoot boy with cheek, blasts through the countryside carrying the flag of Ford and Shelby-American. He and Jerry Grant gave it all they had but the rough roads—built by the Romans thousands of years before—tore up the suspension something awful. Four of the team Cobras broke. Gurney/Grant finished 8th overall and 2nd in GT, but only after the race scorers had gone home! *Ford Motor Co. photograph*

A victory lap somewhere in the U.S. in the 1960s. Bob Johnson, a Shelby team racer, cruises around the track on a victory lap while Peyton Cramer, Shelby's Ivy League General Manager, flies the checkered flag. Note the small Plexiglas wraparound windscreen instead of glass framed metal windshield.

Somewhere in America, a factory competition 289 roadster is flung around a corner. Note the wire grille protector actually protecting the fog lamps as well, but ironically the chicken wire that Shelby originally had in there is missing. The horizontal stripe was a different color on each team's cars so pit crew workers would know which driver was coming into the pits so they could be ready if it was "their" car.

August 1964. Meadowdale Raceway, Illinois. Ken Miles, Shelby's most celebrated driver, is pictured here in the 289 team car reserved for him. There was no more valuable driver to the Shelby-American team than Ken Miles who had been racing even before WWII in his native England. He was hired on at Shelby-American after making a Tiger prototype that met Shelby's approval. He became not only a key team driver, but Shelby's No. 1 development driver on such cars as the 289 Competition car, the 427 Cobra and the Ford GT. His 289 Cobra was set up a bit different than the others including a Heim-jointed suspension. Like Shelby, for some superstitious reason both preferred to run their lucky number "98" in the roundel. Miles was killed testing an experimental Ford GT (the J-car) in 1966. Mike Odell captured Miles at speed in a shot at Meadowdale International raceway in 1964 with a Canon camera. *Mike Odell, SportsRacingLtd.com*

2006, Willow Springs, CA. Today, in the new century, there are legions of new Italian and German cars bearing the latest technology. But the latest collector car auction results show that what the real racers want is Cobra replicas, as much like the 1960s originals as you can make them. Kirkham in Utah makes an aluminum bodied 289 model that fits on top of their coil-spring frame for the best of both worlds—you don't have to run a big block, which makes it lighter and better handling and it's not so intimidating to drive. A big block can get away from you real quick, and then there's hell to pay.

Owners of replica Cobras are becoming astute students of the marque's original history. Here a replica owner has fabricated his own period-style breathers for his steel valve covers that recall the factory originals. Under racing conditions if you don't have breathers, the pressure can blow out the valve cover gaskets.

A tale of two small-blocks. Both sport four twin-choke IDA Webers from Italy, the same carbs as used by Ferrari. The Webers and manifold from Shelby could set you back two grand, which was one third of a down payment on a three bedroom house back then. And the Webers had a nasty habit of belching fire out the top when cold! (One 427 Cobra with Webers was called "Ollie the Dragon" because of its penchant for belching fire out the air scoop when started!) Note: the owner of the car at left is running grooved aluminum valve covers but the Shelby team cars had steel valve covers because when you needed to weld on breather tubes, it was a lot harder to find a guy who could weld aluminum than it was to find someone who could weld steel.

The Mercer Cobra. Does it look prewar? Well that's intentional since this car was born after Virgil Exner, Chrysler's flamboyant inventor of the tail fin. Exner secured a contract from the Copper Development Association to make a one-off show car copying a sketch he had made earlier for an article in *Playboy* magazine. He borrowed design cues from the prewar Mercer sports car, and mounted his design on a lengthened Cobra chassis. It was flamboyant and remains one of the lowest mileage A.C. Cobras in existence.

The headlights were hidden until needed, whereupon they flipped out into place. The car was bodied in Italy by a small coachbuilder. Exner went on to design the first Stutz Blackhawks, also postwar American cars bodied in Italy, featuring prewar classic themes. *Ford Motor Co. photograph*

Ford's Cougar II concept car (they called them dream cars back then) was based on a leaf sprung CSX2008 series chassis and was Ford's attempt to update the Cobra with a "modern" body that would be a fitting rival to Chevrolet's then-oh-so-edgy Sting Ray. It had a fiberglass body plus a brushed metal roof but only one was made because, by the time they got it done, they were already thinking of phasing out the leaf-sprung chassis and going to an all-new coil spring chassis, which meant they would have had to design a new body. *Ford Motor Co. photograph*

Like the Corvette the Cougar II had hidden headlamps. The candy apple red painted car was long thought lost until Cobra historian Jeff Burgy tracked it down. Burgy found it in the storage area of a Detroit museum and talked them into letting him cosmetically renew it along with a sister Cobra concept car for an appearance at a Shelby club convention in nearby Ypsilanti. *Ford Motor Co. photograph*

Monterey Historic 1982. You could consider this car a Shelby, sort of. Shelby claims that the King Cobra (a name conjured up not by Shelby but by the press) came about because back in 1963 the guys at the shop "thought Cobras were production cars and wanted real racecars to work on" so he ordered up three Cooper Monacos from England and fitted Cobra-ized V-8s so they could enter them in United States Road Racing Championship (USRRC) events. The problem was that the Colotti four-speed transaxle from Italy was a notoriously unreliable unit. Ford helped Shelby some in paying development costs but the author thinks the real reason Shelby was racing them was to try to line himself up for the GT40 program which Ford was already working on in 1963. When Ford flopped terribly with the GT40 in 1964, they came hat in hand to Shelby with a plea to make it right. Shelby then abandoned the King Cobras in a nanosecond.

A.C., in England, at first welcomed Shelby with open arms. He was their knight in shining armor, brightening a bleak future! But as time went on, they began to feel a tad shunted off into the background while Shelby gained worldwide fame as the Cobra creator. You might call this car A.C.'s revenge because, reportedly, Shelby had been unaware of A.C.'s own coupe design until it suddenly appeared at a Le Mans practice in April 1964 (aside from newspaper reports after Jack Sears decided to do an impromptu road test on the new M1 motorway and was clocked at over 180 mph, which resulted in speed limits being imposed). This is the same car repaired decades later. During the race it hit a Ferrari, which spun off the track, killing three spectators who had gained entry into a forbidden area. It has since been rebuilt and is a star of British vintage racing. *Barrie Bird photograph*

A Cobra Daytona Coupe is prepared for painting in one of Shelby-American's paint booths, prior to the 24 hours of Le Mans. The body was so soft, one race at an event like Daytona would pit it so terribly that it had to be repainted before the next race. This Grand Touring car is powered by a Ford 289 cubic inch engine, boosted to 385 bhp by Weber carburetion. *Shelby-American, Inc.*

Ford arrives at Le Mans in 1965. The truck with French plates shows how conflicted Ford was in 1965. They would have loved to bring only the mid-engined GTs, which were high tech, but had to bring the Cobra Daytona because it was tried and true. It was a good thing they did, as only the Daytona, of all the factory Fords entered, finished the race! *Bob Negstad Photo*

Monterey Historic in the 1990s. A Cobra Daytona coupe outruns a roadster. The Daytona coupe was basically a roadster with a tubular subframe added to support the coupe body. It could do another 20 mph faster than the roadster with the same engine in the same state of tune. Shelby only built six of them.

Monterey Historic a decade earlier. Here you see two Daytona coupes running side by side, one wearing the light blue 1964 livery and the other the darker 1965 Guardsman Blue color. Back in the 1980s owners ran their Daytonas in vintage racing but today, with any one of the six being worth $4 million plus, it's difficult to talk an owner into getting his car out into the fray where it could get pranged.

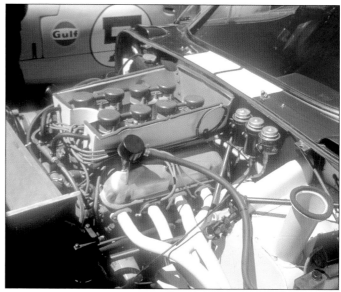

Monterey Historic decades later. Here some restored Cobra Daytona coupes wow the crowd. The coupes squeezed a few more horsepower out of the 289 than the roadsters. Ford's Aeronutronics Division gave aerodynamic advice the second year to dial out some of the mistakes of the originals.

Le Mans 1964. The Cobra Daytona coupe. Basically the Daytona coupe was a Pete Brock design commissioned by Shelby in order to get the Cobra roadster into better aerodynamic shape so it could catch the faster Ferrari GTO coupes. The livery that first year was a pale blue with thin white stripes set wide apart. *Ford Motor Co. photograph*

Le Mans 1965. Yes, this is an original "in period" picture. And, yes, those are original Daytonas in the rented Peugeot garage Ford was using as a race prep shop. Note that one Daytona is painted red—there's an explanation due there: Ford wanted as many Fords in the race as possible and when Shelby found that the Swiss Filipinetti team had a Ferrari entered, but that the car didn't arrive from Modena, he talked them into running a Cobra (and since Count Filipinetti was miffed at Enzo Ferrari he took him up on it). They painted it Ferrari red, maybe to get back at the old man for not sending the promised Ferrari. Alas, the Filipinetti Daytona did not finish.

Italy 1964. Shop Carrozzeria Gran Sport. On the recommendation of Alejandro de Tomaso, Shelby ordered more Cobra Daytona coupes built in Italy because he figured the Italians would be faster bending metal than the Brits. The car in front might be the one at first designated to be a 427 with a longer wheelbase but it was switched back to a 289 when another Daytona was smashed in a trailering accident best summarized as "tall truck/low bridge." *Ford Motor Co. photograph*

Le Mans, 1965. Headlamps and foglamps were taped over in the daytime portions of the race to protect lenses until night when they would be needed.

A modern Shelby coupe. It started out as the "Brock coupe," when Shelby's former employee designed it for the South African kit car maker Superformance. After lawsuits were filed, Superformance and Shelby signed a deal and now it is sold in the U.S. as the "Shelby coupe." It contains numerous improvements over the '64 racing Daytona and will cruise pretty close to 200 mph.

The Willment coupe. Is it a Cobra coupe? Uh, yes, built "in period" with a CSX2000 series chassis number. Is it a Shelby Cobra coupe? Uh, no. Here's the car's *raison d'être*. Sir John Willment was a British car dealer, a Ford dealer no less, and sponsored lots of racecars. Willment contacted Shelby to order a Daytona and was told they didn't have a spare but that they'd send over the plans with a mechanic so that they could build one of their own. The Willment coupe didn't come out looking the same as Shelby's version, though it could indeed hit 170 mph. It won several victories in South Africa.

Sebring 1964. The big block makes its debut in a small block Cobra. That's "The Hawk," AKA Ken Miles, a true Brit, at the wheel. It turns out that Miles wanted to show off his engineering ability and his belief in the old hot rod saying: "There's never enough cubic inches," by shoehorning a 427 FE big-block into a leaf sprung chassis. The result was a car that was squirrelly beyond belief, so much so that in his very first outing in practice for the 12 hours of Sebring, he center-punched a tree square on. He repaired the car, sort of, and co-driver John Morton entered it in the race the next day, only to blow the engine. *Villem Oosthook collection*

Sebring 1964. Don't let those three Ferrari GTO breathing holes fool you—that's the nose of a car born as a small block Cobra. Only this one had a big block 427 in it, shoehorned by Ken Miles who crashed it in practice, and then he stayed up all night to pound it out so John Morton could race it the next day. The car's nickname was "the slug" and when it blew, Morton's terse comment when he arrived at the pits was: "the slug is dead."

Sebring 1965. Nighttime shot refueling the Schlesser/Bondurant coupe. That looks like "Rem," i.e., Phil Remington, filling the car up. Remington, a hot rodder before the war and a flight mechanic on B-17s in England during WWII, came from playboy Lance Reventlow's former Scarab operation to Shelby and proved that he could do every kind of fabrication. He was with Shelby through the whole Cobra and Ford GT program, finally going to Gurney's AAR operation and working another 30-plus years. *Ford Motor Co. photograph*

The press release heading read: "Cobra 289 Gets a big brother." Shelby-American's new 427 Cobra, right, poses alongside the popular 289 Cobra. Body style changes were minor, but underneath it was all new, including a 427 cubic inch Ford engine and coil spring suspension.

This is the street car version, which sometimes was sold with a lower power 428 with the buyer unaware of the switch from the advertised 427 engine.

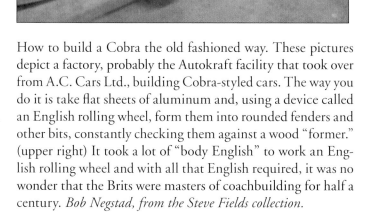

How to build a Cobra the old fashioned way. These pictures depict a factory, probably the Autokraft facility that took over from A.C. Cars Ltd., building Cobra-styled cars. The way you do it is take flat sheets of aluminum and, using a device called an English rolling wheel, form them into rounded fenders and other bits, constantly checking them against a wood "former." (upper right) It took a lot of "body English" to work an English rolling wheel and with all that English required, it was no wonder that the Brits were masters of coachbuilding for half a century. *Bob Negstad, from the Steve Fields collection.*

427 Cobra as film star. The Cobra was a dramatic car and just naturally attracted producers' eyes. Here's a real 427, one of two rented for the movie *Gumball Rally*, loosely based on the real Cannonball Baker Sea-to-Shining-Sea Memorial Trophy Dash conceived by Brock Yates. Michael Sarrazin is at the wheel while a lowly Ferrari Daytona tries to pass. The movie crew pranged one of the cars during the filming but repainted both cars before giving them back to their worried owners. The film's plot is negligible but the Cobra's looks and sounds steal the show!

Chuck Bail, the producer, was a real reality buff so he eschewed the visual blue screen to fake a car running on the road and mounted a real camera to the front of the Cobra so you would see the actual background as the car drove down the road.

Sebring 1965. The 427 Cobra came along just when most successful sports racing cars were coupes. But we just can't help, when looking at the Le Mans start for Sebring in 1965, thinking that the guy in the open 427 Cobra had more fun than all the guys in the closed cars. At least until the point when it started to rain.

Los Angeles, California, 1965. Now those who want to argue that big-block Cobras never came new with twin carbs will have to argue with the man that owns the hand visible in the picture. The carburetors were 650cfm Autolites on an aluminum Shelby manifold. That man is your author, then a fledgling reporter visiting the Shelby factory, on assignment for *Motor Trend*. The author can remember nothing of that visit except Shelby's stunning, tall, blonde, suntanned secretary. *Mike Lamm photograph*

A 427 comp car or S/C's four barrel carb sits in the so-called "turkey pot" because that's the way Shelby insured it breathed only cold air, sealing the top of the alloy enclosure to the hood scoop. Most 427s came with chrome steel valve covers but some street owners prefer aluminum-grooved ones because they proclaimed COBRA 427 in bas-relief letters.

Riverside, California, circa 1965. Carroll Shelby (left) in a blazer he probably later wished he'd hidden, and his sometimes rival, sometimes partner Dan Gurney by the first All-American Eagle, the result of a joint partnership in a firm called All-American Racers. Gurney later won Spa in an Eagle but his biggest success with the marque was in selling a lot of them to Indy racers. Shelby sold out his share of All-American Racers to Gurney early on. *Riverside Raceway Photo*

One of the wildest Daytona coupes was one that in point of fact never turned a wheel in combat for Shelby-American back in the day. That was the Type 65, which Brock talked Shelby into building on the new coil-sprung chassis with a 427 under the hood. Shelby was reluctant, Ford having told him all they wanted to see was Ford GTs but he told Brock to go ahead and designated a British upholsterer to build it. Upholsterer? Yup, you heard that right. The results were awkward, to say the least, and Shelby sold the car unfinished. It was restored decades later and recently sold for over a million dollars.

One of Shelby's last efforts for Ford in the Sixties was to build his own design from the ground up, the fabled Lone Star (named after the motto of Texas, which briefly was an independent republic). It was built in England, with much of the metal work done by Gomm Metal, and adopted the basic configuration of the GT40, being mid-engined with gas tanks on either side. The engine was a 351 and the gearbox a ZF. But Ford was totally disinterested in it, perhaps due to their new emphasis on having Shelby run Trans-Am teams. Or maybe back in Dearborn they had had enough problems with delicate Cobra bodywork to want to fund another car made in England. At any rate, the car was sold off and kicked around until it was rescued by the respected Cobra historian Michael Schoen, who is restoring the car today.

Personalized plates make Cobras lots of fun. But, of course, there is a race down to the DMV each January by Cobra and Cobra replica and Shelby owners to see who can get the most "infra dig" Shelby-related plate.

England, the mid-60's. Ford was miffed with the shabby way stevedors walked on the 289 Cobras when they were shipped by sea, requiring much body repair prior to sale, so shipping 427 Cobras by air was tried. These three big block coil spring Cobras have very early serial numbers, and at least one or two probably went right to Dearborn before they went to Shelby. They were shipped without engines, 427 side oilers being easier to get on the American side of "the pond." *Photo courtesy of Graham Gauld collection*

Dick Smith, Fresno, California, bail bondsman, pictured back in the day in his publicity photo when he was running one of the winningest Cobras ever! Note the full width Plexiglas racing windshield.

Dick Smith's mechanic was Roy Wiley. Smith still proudly owned the car four decades later during which time it increased in value more than 10,000 percent! (Better than most Dow Jones stocks!)

Cobra Day at the Petersen Museum. This was a memorable event produced several times by Cobra maven Lynn Park. Shelby would usually make an appearance and it was like a homecoming to him, seeing so many of the cars he built. This car is the definitive 427 Cobra fitted out the way that everyone likes, with all the bells and whistles including oil cooling scoop with oil cooler, twin radiator pusher fans, chrome side pipes, hood scoop, and chrome roll bar.

Smith's 427 at various events. Smith switched to a street windshield later on so it would be street-legal. He liked the number "198" on the car because his Cobra was clocked at Daytona at that MPH. We speculate it might have been a tad breezy at that point!

Monterey Historics. In repeated visits to Laguna Seca, Dr. Mac Archer shows that even with a big-block Cobra born as a street car (one clue: street cars have glove compartments) you can kick ass on a racetrack against cars more hi-tech, like Porsches. His 427 carried him through many races at Monterey. Unfortunately, local residents began to resent the noise of racecars (duh, that's what you get when you move next to a racetrack), so he now has to run with SuperTrapp mufflers.

This classic 427 has belonged to Tom McIntyre of California for decades. Tom's theory is: "Pretty cars are for the concours but my car's a driver." Many times Tom drove it to events at Riverside or Willow, raced it hard, and drove home. His car is a subtle grey similar to the 2006 Ford GT Tungsten Grey, and shows the "road rash" that the eggshell-thin aluminum body of a Cobra is subject to.

Oakland, California, 1977. The first Shelby-American Automobile Club convention. Your author was there and captured this S/C (no glove compartment) with its comp gas cap with his Hasselblad 500C and telephoto lens. But for an S/C it has a couple non-stock items for that model—a full-width rear bumper from the road car and a non-Cobra dash insignia. But we know the car is real, as replicas weren't yet on the market when this car was out and about.

Here, at Laguna Seca in Monterey, a vintage racing cobra cruises. Note chrome side pipes favored in later years by owners of genuine A.C. Cobras and replica owners.

When Cobras went to private teams the mechanics would sometimes cobble up some-thing that Shelby-American would not have used, such as the rear brake scoop on this big block. But on the other hand, the factory team couldn't complain because other than one or two races run by Miles in a big block, they developed the 427 Cobra and then walked away from it after Ford made it abundantly clear that they wanted all Shelby hands at their battle stations for the Ford GT.

Cobra dashboard. This one not only has the traditional gauge layout, with the tach redlined by the owner at 6000 rpm but a speedometer that reads backwards from right to left (pegging at 180 mph). Someday the mystery of the backwards reading speedom-eters will be solved.

Willow Springs in the 1980s. What did you do with a 427 Cobra before vintage racing began to take hold? Try Solo One, the practice of one car at a time touring a racetrack to see if it can beat its own time. The roll bar in this real 427 is ugly but no doubt more effective than the hoop type. Note the added front spoiler. At right the same owner tries a slalom. The technique best used with a 427 Cobra was "point and squirt."

Cobra Day at the Petersen Museum. Los Angeles, California, in the early 2000s. Cobra collector Lynn Park organized several of these events which resulted in a record of 10 percent of the original production of Cobras showing up. Here you see one 427 with a chrome roll bar while the other has a black roll bar but even the Shelby team cars had both finishes at different times. Even the comp gas caps seem different; one was sunk more into the body than the other. You have to figure though, over 40 years, many of the 998 A.C. Cobras originally made back then have since been modified, painted, customized, and redone (not to mention the ones crashed and rebuilt) so many times that it's difficult to know what "correct" is.

What's one of the rarest big-block Cobras you can think of? Try one with dry sump, indicated here by the extra filler cap on the right front fender. Shelby had the package developed—which retailed for around $2000—but no one wanted it because the 427 Cobra failed to get homologated in 1965 as a production sports car. When the FIA inspector showed up to count cars Shelby was dozens of cars short. So the result was that Ford didn't fund any budget for Shelby-American to race the 427 Cobra, at that point concentrating on getting the Ford GT to straighten up and fly right.

Thames-Ditton England 1965. Here's what the Brits laughingly called an assembly line. One phrase you didn't dare mention in Jollie Olde England was "line speed" as they were lucky to make 15 cars a week where Ford in Detroit could make 60 per hour on any one assembly line. And do not begrudge them the two obligatory halts for the daily cuppa. British tradition, y'know. Way in back, on the same line, you see an invalid carrier that was A.C.'s mainstay for many decades. To think they made some of the slowest vehicles in the world and at the same time some of the fastest!

Oakland, California, 1977. Yes, it's a real 427 Cobra, replicas had not yet populated the land. Note the two taillights on each side, yet no one seems able to explain 40-plus years later why some big-block Cobras had two taillights and others a single vertical lens per side. It might have been to conform to regulations in different countries. Color here was Barris-painted Candy Pearl.

Here's a close up of a racing Cobra that needs some answer: why the mesh? Maybe to relieve air pressure from forcing open the trunk lid at speed. Shelby never developed the 427 Cobra as much as the 289 because they rarely raced it as a factory racecar. Gurney, when asked if he'd rather race a 289 or 427 told the author without hesitation in 2006, "A 289—because the big block would run out of brakes long before the small block."

Godzilla's ride. Shelby built the ultimate Cobra for himself in the 1960s. It was equipped with a 427 side oiler and an MX Lincoln 3-speed automatic and, get this, twin Paxtons, which pumped it up to around 800 hp. It would do about 175 mph. He blew the engine once on his way to Elko, Nevada, and left it sitting by the side of the road as he hitched a ride so he could get to the party in Elko. Later a songwriter bought it. The IRS was after the car because the songwriter didn't pay taxes and finally it was sold through an ad in *Hemmings Motor News*. Harley Cluxton sold it at an auction in 2007 for $5.5 million. An identical car was built for comedian Bill Cosby that was wrecked and had its chassis replaced in the rebuild. The interior had extra gauges to monitor the twin Paxtons. Shelby liked lots of gauges, owing to being a test pilot during the war. No doubt some Cobra replica owners will try to build the same twin Paxton set-up but they should be mindful of the fact that a man driving the Cosby car was killed when it got away from him. As it turns out, there can be too much power!

Derek Hurlock of A.C. Cars Ltd. poses with their version of the coil spring chassis. Just as they had previously sold leaf-spring 289 Cobras, A.C. wrangled permission from Shelby to sell coil-spring chassis in the U.K. but this time opted for a measure of rationality by selling their version with the small-block engine in the coil-spring chassis and going back to wire wheels (which Shelby wouldn't dare use in a 427-powered version as it might snap the spokes). Shelby probably figured that it was no skin off his nose, as who would want a small block when they could get a big block? Some buyers of this model, called an A.C. 289, later switched the engine to a 427 on their own, making a car that, DNA-wise, is pretty near 99 percent A.C. Cobra. It's close—but no-cigar in value since it lacks the all-important CSX3000-series serial number that makes a 427 Cobra as good as gold. *Ford Motor Co. photograph*

The A.C. 289 had a 427 Cobra tube frame chassis, a 427 Cobra's coil springs, but a 289 engine. That was because the Hurlocks decided that that the thundering 427 was too much of a gas-guzzler for the UK and Continental market. Once they had a smaller engine, they could safely bring back the wire wheels which wouldn't have stood the torque of the big blocks. Less than 30 AC289s were built, some in LHD. They had a different serial number sequence than the CSX3000 Cobras made in America and were never marketed as "Cobras."

Ford's styling boss, Eugene Bordinat, was a bit jealous of his counterpart, William L. Mitchell, vice president in charge of Styling at GM, who was always ordering up custom cars built as his own personal toys. So Bordinat had a Cobra coil-spring chassis fitted with this body, called the XD Cobra officially (but the "Bordinat Cobra" behind his back). The body was made of a rubber-like material called "Royalex" where small dents would pop out with the application of heat. Only one was built. It still exists today, unrestored, and resides in deep storage at a Detroit museum.

The dashboard of the XD Cobra shows an attempt by Detroit car designers to make some sense out of the A.C. Cobra dashboard. First of all there was no place on the A.C. Cobra dash for a radio. How are you going to add those high profit items for the dealers if there's no place for a radio? So that was included. Gauges appear to be Smiths. Ford would have undoubtedly offered it with an automatic.

Did someone say "Stingray?" Ford would have liked to put the XD Cobra into production but by the time this car was built, Ford could see the end of Cobra production coming, and the technology for the body material was still too experimental.

The Bordinat Cobra had a lift-off hardtop as well.

AC introduce the 427 chassis

backbone of the new AC 427 Convertible

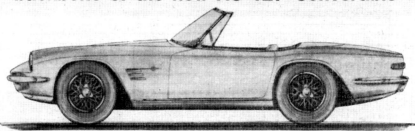

Coachwork for both the AC 427 Convertible and the Cobra 427 is built on this chassis which is shown at Earls Court for the first time. Specifications include four wheel independent suspension with double wishbones and coil springs incorporating race car principles; all of which in turn provide exceptional stability coupled with maximum comfort.

Shelby American fit the 7-litre Ford V-8 engine to the Cobra 427. The wheelbase is extended by 6 inches for the AC 427

Convertible and when fitted with the 7-litre engine provides a car giving fantastic performance.

The following cars will be on view at Earls Court on Stand 109:

AC 427 Convertible
AC 289
Cobra 427 (in full racing trim)

and the latest Cobra

A.C. CARS LTD. Thames Ditton, Surrey. Telephone: Emberbrook 5621 Telegrams: 'Autocarrier, Thames Ditton'

A.C. Cars Ltd. also regarded the original Cobra's eggshell-thin body as a problem (it didn't help that stevedores walked on the cars when they first tried shipping by sea) so they had Frua, in Italy, design a more svelte design in steel. This ad was prepared when they still thought they were going to build it with a 427.

But by the time orders started to come in A.C. decided that engine was too much of a brute and went for a 428, and the aluminum body was changed to a steel one. Roughly 86 were sold, counting both coupe and convertible forms, but there was no U.S. spec model. It was available in left-hand drive for continental countries and right-hand drive for the U.K. One of the magazines said it was a great rival to the Maserati Ghibli and you had to consider it cost much less to maintain than an Italian GT.

The AC428 roadster bares strong resemblance to some Italian-made Maseratis and no wonder—the designers were Frua, the coachbuilding firm in Italy also doing some Maseratis at the time. *Photo courtesy of AC Owners Club UK*

The AC428 coupe was a close competitor to the Maserati Ghibli coupe. You could describe it as a car with "lazy power." in that the 428 engine didn't have to strain at all to get it up to 165 mph. It was available with an automatic. AC built both the roadster and coupe on stretched versions of the 427 Cobra chassis. The sales were sabotaged by an oil shortage in the early '70s, compounded by slow deliveries from Italy. *Photo courtesy of AC Owners Club UK*

Palm Springs Vintage Races, the mid 1980s. Yes, your eyes do not deceive you, that's Der Snakemeister himself in one of the most controversial Cobras ever to turn a wheel. Shelby called it a "continuation car," claiming he had come across some uncompleted 427 Cobra chassis in one of his facilities that he intended to build out as finished cars. He registered that first one with the California DMV, using a serial number recorded after that used by the last Cobra built in the 1960s. At the event Shelby practiced in a GT350 but wisely didn't run the race in either car because he said he could see a lot of racers with engines tweaked way beyond 1960s specs itching to "blow off the old man." Bear in mind that Shelby still had major heart difficulties at the time (his transplants were still ahead of him). The Cobra continuation car didn't run the event. Nobody knows how many of the continuation cars were built, estimates are anywhere from five to ten. Selling prices were close to $500,000!

Here's a Shelby CSX 4000 car that's been polished out. Shelby liked it so much he even borrowed the car back from the owner to display at Monterey. Though blinding on a sunny day, having an unpainted aluminum body is one way to set your Cobra replica apart from the sea of fiberglass-bodied replicas encountered at most Shelby events.

This Shelby CSX4000 replica belongs to a Southern gentleman. This owner even has two Shelby-made replicas; one for street driving, the other for racing. Note how the owner has "period correct" decals which give it an authentic look, but that's somewhat mitigated by more modern modular wheels, which weren't available in the sixties.

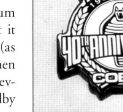

And wouldn't you know, you can't have aluminum around for long before some fool starts going at it with the Brillo pads, polishing it to lower the drag (as was done with racing airplanes before the war). When Shelby dreamed up his 40th Anniversary Cobra, several customers ordered theirs polished out. Shelby should have supplied a set of Ray-Bans!

Bengt-Ace Gustavsson of Sweden (www.racefoto. se) captured this car on film at a race in Sweden. It is owned and raced by Bengt Johansson from Kalmar, in southeast Sweden. It is an excellent example of a "home built" Cobra that only in its spirited performance and body shape does it continue the Cobra revolution that Shelby started. Gustavsson bought the body from a local company and made the chassis himself. The engine is an old Corvette 350 with what he estimates is 500 bhp. The gearbox is a Muncie (GM) M22 "rock crusher." The suspension is from a Corvette. The engine has a Holley 750 carburetor. Why the front spoiler? Well, Gustavsson reports that the first time he put the car on the track "it became very unstable when he passed 140 mph!" Now with a front spoiler at the Formula 1 track, Anderstorp, he clocks nearly 170 mph. He won the Swedish championship for modified sportscars in 2001, 2003 and 2005. Coincidentally, Gustavsson reports there only is one real Cobra in Sweden, which happens to be in the garage of King Carl XVI Gustav, the reigning monarch.

The aluminum-bodied A.C. Mk. IV was built in England to U.S. road specifications. It looked a lot like the 427 Cobras except the engine was a fuel-injected 5.0 liter Mustang engine and it had an all-new dashboard design with rocker switches instead of the familiar toggles. One characteristic of the Mk. IV styling was an aluminum shield on the rear fender flares to stop pitting from gravel. A few were ordered without engines and "Cobraized" with a 427 engine.

A.C. Cars has again risen from the ashes and once again is marketing their own rival to Shelby's Cobras. They moved lock, stock and barrel to Malta in the mid-2000s. The early cars produced were prototypes, and production quality is expected to improve. The A.C. MkV was a new model in 2006 and though they do not refer to it as a Cobra, it obviously has many common features with Cobras of the past. The car has to comply with current regulations, which has necessitated a number of design changes to the build specs. Many of their previous MkIV and CRS donor components are now obsolete and have therefore had to be replaced with modern equivalents. According to an A.C. spokesman: "We have upgraded the car mechanically with the selection of new high-performance brakes and the addition of power steering, initially on the RGD variant." Note how the wheels no longer have knock-offs, those being against the law in some countries, including the U.S. The dashboard is considerably redesigned from the A.C. Cobra days. The V-8 is now sourced from Lotus.

Alan Lubinsky, a south African entrepreneur, bought A.C. Cars Ltd. and moved it around a bit from country to country until he decided what to do with it. At one point in the early 2000s Shelby and A.C. announced that A.C. would be building cars for America and this picture of a nicely polished car was released by A.C. but then the deal fell apart, much to the disappointment of traditionalists who would have loved to have an A.C.-Shelby Cobra available once again. *Photo courtesy Alan Lubinsky*

Jay Leno is Los Angeles car supremo when it comes to collecting, and one would think that when he orders a Cobra it would be a real CSX3000 car. But Leno told the author that he ordered a replica built by Mark Gerish of Wisconsin because he wanted one "he wouldn't have to worry about."

There's nothing vintage race fans like more than to see a former Champion come back and take a few laps in one of his old racecars. In this case the car was a birdcage Maserati and the pilot no less than Carroll Shelby, who won many races in the birdcages in his final seasons. They were called "birdcages" because with the aluminum bodywork off the shape of the frame's tubing looked like a birdcage. This was at the Monterey Historic before Shelby's first heart transplant so you know what a chance he was taking to please his fans who wanted to once again see him drive a racecar.

Shelby is back in racing, sort of. This is the Challenge car he displayed at the Fabulous Fords Forever show at Knott's Berry Farm in 2007. The "Challenge" is and open track endurance event where you race at seven tracks in seven days. Note how high the padded roll bar is. The dashboard has all new modern style gauges but overall the car still reflects the Cobras of the sixties.

A 1963 Mustang perhaps? Yes, this concept car was seen tooling about the auto show circuit and various racetracks as a pace car in 1963, so since the 1964 Mustang hadn't been introduced yet, we'll call it a 1963 that used a 1964's customized body shell. It was called the Mustang II and had more adventurous lines than the stock Mustang. The removable hardtop was an idea revived decades later by Ford on a production Mustang. Ford later donated the car to the Owl's Head Museum. *Ford Motor Co. photograph*

Greenfield Village Sports Car Show 1964. No, your eyes do not deceive you. What we have here is a shortened wheelbase two-seater Mustang made from a 2+2. Ford didn't explain why custom fabricator Andy Hotten of Dearborn Steel Tubing built this car, but speculation today is that either it was some Ford executive ordering it for himself on a whim or it was a stalking horse for the later Shelby Mustang. So, though none ever reached production, the two-seat Mustangs showed that Ford management was willing to consider a special Mustang, and that's why the GT350 got "green lighted" so quickly. Shelby made it a two-seater by simply removing the rear seat, no cutting necessary.

The first GT350 street model prototype. Note the decal on the front fender, which was not used in production. The wheels were subcontracted from Cragar and are chromed steel rims with aluminum centers. *Ford Motor Co. photograph*

Production of the Cobra and Shelby Mustang GT350 was carried out in Shelby-American's 12.5-acre facility on the south side of Los Angeles International Airport. The plant was flanked on the left in this aerial photo by West Imperial road and the right by the airport main runway. The Pacific Ocean is in the background a couple miles west. All those cars on the right are unpainted, unsold 427 Cobras that failed to get homologated as production sports cars in 1965.

Shelby-American assembly of the Cobra and Shelby Mustang GT350 began with raw stock, pictured here. In the foreground are fastback Mustangs from the Ford Mustang plant in San Jose, California, which arrived with special deletions to be replaced by Shelby-American components enroute to becoming full-fledged GT 350s. In the background are aluminum-bodied 427 Cobras awaiting parts like precious Halibrand wheels.

Street Mustangs passed along the production pit on their way to becoming Shelby GT350 Mustangs. Here the front geometry was altered, suspension beefed up and special engine equipment added. A tuned header exhaust system is about to be installed in this photograph.

Los Angeles Airport "snake works" factory, 1965. In the foreground is the only big-block prototype built on a leaf-spring chassis, number 2196. After it was crashed by Miles at Nassau, it was built into the "flip-top" as pictured. The car was as ill-handling as the first big block prototype so Shelby decided to have Ford design an all-new coil spring chassis for the big block.

In the west end of the competition shop, an area was set aside for the GT350 R-models to be assembled. When finished, the GT350 was transformed into a full competition "B" production racecar.

Note the R-model's poor-fitting aluminum side window frames and the front fiberglass "apron" which functioned as an air scoop for the radiator. Roughly 36 R-models were made.

Freshly completed Shelby Mustangs await rail and truck delivery to franchised Shelby-American dealers across the nation. Shelby claimed in their press releases that they could make 150 GT 350 cars per month. Shelby-American operated its own fleet of auto transporters as part of its national distribution system.

This shot of a black 1966 GT350 shows how slick a vintage Shelby can be in your basic black. Ford offered the 1966 Shelbys in several colors including black, green, and red.

Most of the 1965-66 GT350s are still on the road some four decades later. This one has been modified six ways to Sunday and it's a pleasure to see such high tech bits as the Heim-jointed aluminum links taking the place of the low cost stamped steel export brace. This car has a Roush-sourced radiator and probably a Roush-sourced engine, if you believe the decals. Roush is a sort of modern day Shelby, with many parallels including, like Shelby, augering a WWII plane into the turf.

Fontana, California, 2005. A 1965 R-model, easily identified by pop-rivets on the aluminum replacing the heavy Ford roof louvers and the aluminum window frames. Shelby made less than 40 but there are several clones out there today, the real ones being almost too valuable to vintage race.

The R-model racing Shelby gas tank was made by welding two regular Mustang gas tanks into one big one. The spout is to catch gas that spills out to the side when you are filling it in one heap of a hurry.

The wheels on the R-model were very lightweight, made of magnesium (not aluminum) by American Racing. They measured 7-in. x 15-in. The originals are hard to find but you can buy aluminum replicas that look virtually identical.

The dash of the R-model dispensed with all regular Mustang gauges, Shelby preferring something that worked under race conditions. Note the old racer's trick of tilting the tach to the right so that at redline the needle reads straight up and your addled brain can get the message that much faster.

The R-model rear windscreen was another genius Brock idea—he wanted more air in the interior so he made it so that the Plexiglas rear window didn't come all the way to the top. Some also figure his design had some aerodynamic advantage.

A more stock looking engine in a Shelby Mustang. This has the stock Monte Carlo bar joining the two shock towers to minimize body flex, something Ford first learned about when their rally car subcontractor, Alan Mann, added them when prepping Falcons for the Monte Carlo rally in Europe. Shelbys came stock with grooved valve covers in 1965 and 1966. By far the most important part of any 1960s Shelby, though, is the pop-riveted aluminum plate that identifies it as a Shelby with the all-important serial number. Today resto shops will sell you a blank of that same plate to complete your ground-up restoration, but you best not punch a number into it that's not your car's number, or else the FBI might come knocking.

One of the most stalwart independent competitors in a Shelby GT350 was Dave Dralle, whose engine building skills are legendary. Now he has a shop right on site at Willow Springs International Raceway, ironically right where some of the original Shelbys were test driven over 40 years ago.

Son of Dracula's ride. Bela Lugosi Jr.'s car was this street Shelby with an R-model front valance panel. Since his father was famous for playing the role of Count Dracula in films, his personalized license plate, DRAQLA, reflected that connection.

Question: What would a 1965-66 Shelby look like without stripes? Answer: See this one photographed in 2006 at a Shelby meet. A good many were shipped that way and the stripes added at the dealer level. This one has an R-model front valance panel.

Los Angeles, California, 1965. A prototype Paxton supercharger. Shelby knew about superchargers, they were offered on super luxury cars like the Duesenberg SJ and Blower Bentleys before the war. And they were on some of the engines of airplanes he test flew during the war. It is said that Paxton built a modified Shelby and brought it over to show Carroll Shelby. Shelby was dubious until the Paxton rep challenged him to a race, Shel in a Cobra. When the blown Shelby won, it got Shelby's attention. This early blower case is rather flat compared to the one they finally used. *Photo courtesy Paradise Wheels*

This is another experimental version of the blower with a flat grooved, removable top to the air box. Shelby planned to make many supercharged ones at his factory but it ended up being mostly a dealer-installed option. Shelby also greatly reduced the warranty period when you ordered a blower, so that gives you an idea of how much peril it put the engine in. *Photo courtesy Jeff Burgy*

A production Paxton supercharger. Shelby promised a 46 percent power increase for the $670 option. Shelby eventually ordered over 500 Paxton kits for 1966 models. The supercharged GT350s got Autolite 4100 4V carbs and Carter high-volume fuel pumps. Inside, supercharged cars got Paxton gauges for the manifold pressure and vacuum, both mounted in a chrome bezel underneath the dash center.

Just one sign of how gung ho Shelby fans are is how some go to great lengths to have all the period-correct decals laid on. This one boasts the usual complement plus the Terlingua racing team—one that alludes to the mythical team that Shelby and his cohorts thought up in order to promote some desert scrubland they were trying to unload down in Texas. They also thought up a chili cookout to promote the land and the cook-offs became international events with Shelby eventually entering the chili preparations market with his own mix.

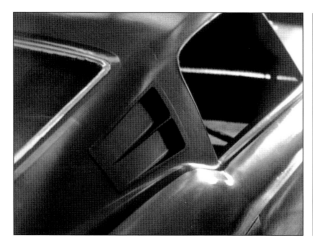

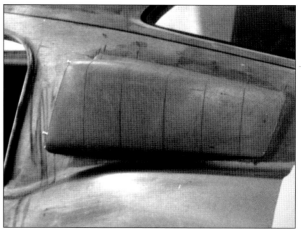

A side scoop detail. Some brain thought it would be cute to set a colored aircraft light in the roof scoop to make the Shelby distinctive. Only after the cars were out on the market did Shelby discover that this was illegal in most states; red lights are only allowed on the sides of vehicles if you are a policeman or fireman.

Chuck McHose was a young designer that Ford assigned out of Dearborn to go to the Shelby works in 1966 to design the 1967 Shelby. Using a body shell from a pre-production prototype they laid on the clay following Shelby's constant admonitions to "make the nose longer." Shelby relished the chance to make a car different from the regular Mustang.

The 1967 Shelby at first had a pair of headlamps located close together in the grille which looked real sexy but Shelby was unaware this arrangement ran afoul of the law in several states. Later in the model run, they were moved further outboard to satisfy authorities in the affected states.

By the time the 1967 Shelbys came around, Ford was no longer promoting the Shelby in racing so there weren't any 1967 factory race Shelbys built by the Shelby works. That left it up to Shelby owners. Here is one built decades later by JBA Racing in San Diego, California.

Shelby with the 1967. The 1967 models required a lot of handwork, as the fiberglass didn't quite fit because the body shell used as the basis when designing the fiberglass bits had been a bit wonky to start with. In mid-1967 production shifted to A.O. Smith in Michigan.

These are not Shelby Mustangs per se but they were built into racecars by Shelby and engineered by Shelby's engineers like Chuck Cantwell. Trans Am racing required a different car than a Shelby Mustang. Shelby built at least 16, and they were rode hard and put away wet, which explains why so few survived.

Here's a Mustang wearing the livery of the yellow and black painted Terlingua Racing Team that Shelby's Trans Am notchback wore in 1967.

This '67 owner is protecting the lights with adhesive tape. Note shoulder harnesses—stock on Shelby's in 1967.

The 1968 Shelbys were like the 1967s except that the hood scoop was moved forward to where it had a chance of actually catching some air. In addition, the taillights were changed to Thunderbird units, and there was a convertible. By 1968, Shelby production had been farmed out to a firm called A.O. Smith in Michigan, which had just finished building the 1967 Corvettes.

A 1968 Shelby Mustang with the French-made *tres chic* Marchal fog lamps. Apparently, Shelby's wish to add a continental flair to his cars went afoul, with the Marchals failing left and right. There was eventually a recall so they could substitute them with Lucas Square 8s, which were not much better. Any fan of English cars could have told them that Joseph Lucas was commonly referred to as "the prince of darkness."

The convertible top in the 1968 Shelby had a thin glass rear window that folded in the middle when the top went down.

The 1968 Shelby convertible. It had a padded roll bar. This is the prototype which accounts for some trim items that don't match the production parts.

A 1968 Shelby cruises down a street in Glendale, California, during a muscle car tribute.

In the 1968s, the big blocks are favored in the collector car sweepstakes, especially the Cobra Jet 428s, which came into the 1968 model year late. They wore badges that said "KR" for "King of the Road."

Ford, ever mindful of the day when they would be without the head snake or cowpoke leading up the heard, developed a new muscle car called the Boss 302, the first year of which was 1969. Shelby got a contract to have his company race the Boss 'stangs. The Boss 302, performance-wise, was more like the original '65 GT350s than the later Shelbys.

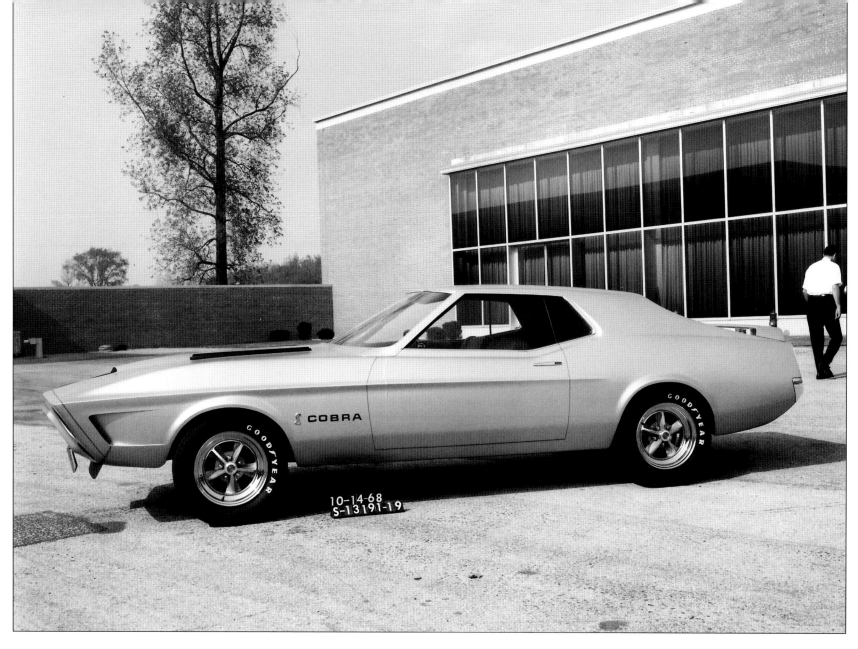

In a weak moment, probably after downing a tall drink, Shelby granted ownership of the name "Cobra" to Ford for the princely sum of one American dollar. Ford began to run with it in 1968 by plastering it all over the Shelby Mustang. As this bizarre clay model shows, they were planning on producing a Cobra-badged Mustang into the early 1970s. But then Bunkie Knudsen was hired from GM and he and Shelby were on the outs. Bunkie backed the "Boss" Mustang and pretty soon Ford didn't need Shelby-branded Mustangs anymore.

Shelby with the 1969 models. From a high view it is easy to see how two of the top vents were air extractors. Every single convertible had the rollover bar.

The 1969 model came standard with mag wheels but for a while there, as this styling prototype shows, Ford was considering mag wheel-styled hubcaps. Horrors!

The most beautiful part of the 1969 and 1970 Shelbys is the cast aluminum exhaust tips, which, unfortunately for a brief time period, were prone to lighting the rear of the car on fire until they changed the gas cap venting.

The convertible of 1969-70 was really a well-designed shape with the long hood and short rear deck that always says "sports car." Note the name on the plate, i.e., "Shelby Cobra." It took Shelby about two more decades before he began to realize that he had given away the farm when he cavalierly sold that name to Ford for a single dollar.

The 1969 and 1970 Shelbys had the most distinctive styling of all the Shelbys in what will probably be called by historians "The First Shelby Mustang Era." That was because Shelby at last got enough budget from Ford to totally re-do the nose and tail so it would be more difficult to spot the car's Mustang origins. Larry Shinoda, who had come over to Ford with his mentor "Bunkie" Knudsen, claimed he designed the car, which copied his Mustang Milano show car. Ironically, while other Mustangs were getting the high winding 351 Cleveland, the Shelby Mustangs got the "old" 351 Windsor, not such a lively engine by comparison. The padded roll bar on the convertible was standard. Ford sort of torpedoed Shelby's sales by introducing the rip-roarin' Boss 302 Mustang in 1969, a car which was much like the '65 Shelby in performance. That left Shelby with so many leftover '69s that Shelby added hood stripes, a front spoiler and newly minted serial numbers (with the permission of the FBI) to make the leftover '69s into 1970 models.

By the time Shelby Mustang production moved to Michigan, there were no factory R-models. But that didn't stop Shelby fans from making them out of the last body style, and here's one from Gordon Gimble, a long time Shelby restorer.

Shelby tried twice in the 1970s and 1980s to partner with someone who could bring back a GT350 clone; but each time the cost of labor, the cost of parts, and the cost of a non-rusty donor car was more than the market could bear once a profit was tacked on. Then a funny thing happened. Hollywood re-made a B-movie called *Gone in 60 Seconds* where the heroic villain lusts after a customized Shelby Mustang. Presto, chango, and suddenly it was okay to mix and match, and to create a Shelby-like car that was far from an original. Shelby got into business with Unique Performance, a Texas firm, making clones of the movie's 1967 Shelby, called "Eleanor," just like the car Nicolas Cage lusted after in the movie.

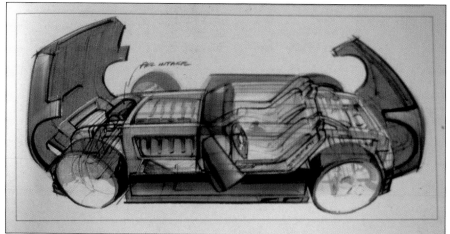

The author feels the Cobra concept roadster of 2002 got a bum rap in that it was actually a totally modern design that is a logical evolution of what would have evolved had the 1960s design stayed in production during the last four decades. Cobra traditionalists panned it, saying it didn't look "Cobra enough" mainly because the grille cavity wasn't an oval shape. Here are some styling sketches showing how they arrived at the final shape. Amazingly, it used much of the 21st century production Ford GT space frame chassis though the '05-'06 Ford GT was a mid-engined car.

Building the Cobra concept roadster. The car was a running, driving car. Doug Gaffka, in charge of the project, said it was the essence of Cobra, not intended to be a copy of the original. J. Mays, head of styling, didn't want it to look too much like the old Cobra for fear that, at the roll-out at the Detroit auto show, reporters would ask: "Why are you showing us a kit car?"

Despite the rejection by the public of the roadster, Ford forged ahead on the Cobra trail and in 2004 unveiled this daring design for a coupe they called the GR-1, again consulting Shelby and having Der Snakemeister himself unveil it at Pebble Beach. The designer was George Saridakus, a young Greek-born designer. It had Lambo-style flip-up doors.

The 2005 Mustang brought back hints of the 1966 Shelby design, particularly in the rear three-quarter windows.

Then Ford showed a GT500 prototype using a supercharged V-8 engine. Some assumed it was a detuned Ford GT engine but there were many differences. Among them was the fact that the 2005-06 Ford GT used a Lysholm supercharger, more precisely made and more efficient than the Roots-type on the 2007 Shelby. But still Ford rated the '07 GT500 at 500 hp, which is nothing to sneeze at. Within a year tuner Roush was promising upgrades that would get you over 700 hp!

The front appearance of the 2007 GT500 was more brutal than the stock Mustang, mostly because of the over-and-under grille cavity. The Plexiglas-protected headlights look like they are painted on, like on a Funny Car.

Before he joined Ford, J. Mays dropped out of car designing for a while to study marketing and brand name imaging, and was convinced that car fans liked a car with a story (in the movie business they call this a back story). So he dipped into Ford's storied past and advocated that Ford make a deal with Hertz to bring back a Hertz Shelby, just like they had 40 years before. Predictably, within weeks of hitting the rental lots across America, the new Hertz Shelbys were showing up at racetracks everywhere, much to the chagrin of Hertz rental managers!

The prototype 2007 GT500 had the SHELBY letters spaced across the rear but the production model had the lettering to one side.

A GT-H rental car. Ford said they would only make 500 for the year 2007 but didn't close the door firmly on whether they would make more in later years. The GT-Hs, unlike the '07 Shelby GT500 models, were actually made in Shelby's Las Vegas factory. The GT-H had its S-H-E-L-B-Y lettering spread out on the rear deck lid like the prototype Shelby GT500.

The bas-relief Cobra emblem, designed way back in 1967 for the Shelby Mustang (left), was updated in the 21st Century by Ford for the new GT500 (right). Ford used the snake emblem on the auto show brochures as well. It started to look a lot like the Viper's snake logo, which must have amused Chrysler designers.

The '07 Shelby includes the GT500 convertible, which, oddly, did not come with hood and tail stripes from the factory.

Three treasures from the Shelby American Collection. Number 21 is CSX 2345, one of the original five 289 FIA roadsters. It boasts no less than five 1st place FIA wins to its credit. In non-FIA-sanctioned events, sometimes roadsters were run with a wraparound plexiglass racing windscreen for the driver only. The Daytona coupe displayed is CSX2299, known as "Gurney's coupe" because it had a taller roofline than the previous ones (due to a mismeasurement by the Italians bodying it) and the 6-foot plus Gurney fit in it better.

Shelby and his "British import" wife, Cleo, sign autographs at the Shelby-American Collection, a museum in Boulder, Colorado.

At the Shelby-American Collection in Boulder, Colorado, visitors see genuine A.C. Cobras from the sixties. The Collection has become a depository for Shelby lore and runs a race team that puts their cars on the grid at vintage events in the U.S. and Europe.

RACING

More Great Titles From Iconografix

All Iconografix books are available from direct mail specialty book dealers and bookstores worldwide, or can be ordered from the publisher. For book trade and distribution information or to add your name to our mailing list and receive a **FREE CATALOG** contact:

Iconografix, Inc.
PO Box 446, Dept BK
Hudson, WI, 54016

Telephone: (715) 381-9755,
(800) 289-3504 (USA),
Fax: (715) 381-9756
info@iconografixinc.com
www.iconografixinc.com

*This product is sold under license from Mack Trucks, Inc. Mack is a registered Trademark of Mack Trucks, Inc. All rights reserved.

More great books from **Iconografix**

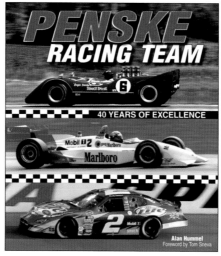
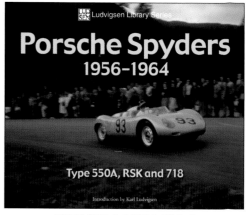

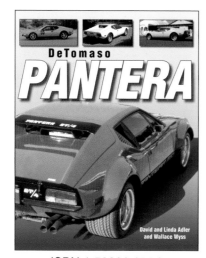
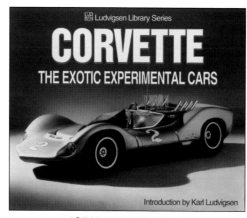
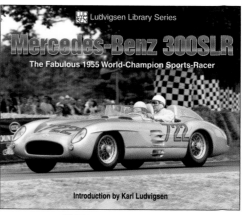